An evening with me

By Jared Stegall

ISBN: 978-1-387-02484-1

DEDICATION

I would like to dedicate this book to Michelle Chambers, Michelle has helped put together both of my poetry books. I also want to say, thanks to all my family and friends for believing in me.

An evening with me was written so you could see just what is going on inside my mind. Because I love my children dearly, my feelings come from the times we shared as they were growing up. There are also those times were it kills me to know how far apart we all are and the less I will get to share the rest of my life with them. So please grab a book and get inside my head to see the journey I have had and continue to have with my friends and family.

There was a time

There was a time,
when you were mine!
Now you belong to him,
starting a family of your own!

There was a time,
when you were mine!
Daddy's little girl, you were
my little butterfly princess!

There was a time,
when you were mine!
How time was flown by,
now you're all grown up!

There was a time,
when you were mine.
I now know, what I must do,
even though I don't want to!

There was a time,
I knew what to do,
but now it's up to you.

I know you're my little girl,
but in order to give you the world
I must let you go.
Please take care of yourself
and know I love you so!
You will always be,
my butterfly princess!

Daddy's little princess

**Touched deeply,
and completely.
Her love is now his.**

**Over time they searched,
through life's
unforeseen journeys.
Even from afar,
I could feel her in my heart.**

**Driven by destiny,
the two will be merged as one.
The love between a
father and daughter,
a bond that will last forever!**

**Even though we are miles apart,
our love cannot
be torn apart!
For Daddy's Little Princess
She will always be...**

Meaningless

Like a storm,
we blow in, we blow out!

Memories like the rain,
absorbed by everything.

If our journey was to end,
without us hand in hand
life would be meaningless!

Without you in it,
my love!

Mother nature's love

Smooth winds blowing
through the mountain pass.

Carrying the sweet aroma of
one who's crossed it path.

Like the queen of all flowers,
her beauty is admired.

Heart beats like thunder,
tears like rain,
enrich the ground beneath.

Her smile has touched God's heart so,
he gave us sunshine.

Eyes filled with love and happiness.

From this point on
I knew her love would last!

Wondering spirits

Lost, with
no words to say.

Then found,
I will not be.

Wondering unseen,
as I walk between,
the living and dead.

She will always be there

**One that smiles,
every day...
Never to let you go,
even when you say...
I don't need you,
please go away...**

**She knows,
when you're happy,
and when you're sad...
She will always be there,
even when you're mad...
When you feel like giving up,
she will never let you down...**

**As beautiful as can be,
but never will she use
it to get her way...**

**When you yell help,
she is the first one you see...
As time goes by just close your eyes
and believe!**

Wronged

So many women
in need of help!
Yet their cries go
unheard no doubt!

Where is the world,
when our daughters
call for help?

I often wonder
when I'm gone,
what will happen
to my little girl,
when she calls out?

I will turn down
heaven, in order
to put that SOB
there in Hell!

Our daughters need us!
What do you say?
Would you help?
Abuse is such an ugly thing
and yet it happens
all the same!

Why do we let this go on,
are we afraid?
Get off your ass
be a real MAN!

Or are you one of
them that sit on

their ass and does nothing?

It's sad,
if you are a dad,
then you know our daughters
come first.

Next time you see
abuse, be a father
don't let it go any
farther.
Love your daughters

A new day

The sun is rising
with her golden rays,
touching the ground.

Shinning down
on our little town.

Road of gold,
paved in brick.

A piece of mind
to know,
she didn't forget.

It's a new day,
she has given us!

A day of peace

A morning on the lake,
peaceful as can be,
just my pole and me.

With the soft warm breeze
and the sun at my back,
let's start this day
off with one hell of a blast.

The greatest fight of the day,
is always in the morning.
For this is when the
fish like to play.

No technology to ruin my day!
For this is a day of peace,
out on the lake!

A Friend's Love

You came into my life,
You made me whole again.
I couldn't have asked
for a better PA or friend.

Now I have someone
I can talk to and be me,
Not the one I pretend to be.

My heart aches for those
who don't get to know love
I guess it's better than being alone,
like me.

If not for my friends
I wouldn't know love.
So, I do understand,
so much.
I guess over the year's
loss was the only life I knew.

Being hurt, I can't take it no more!
Maybe one day before I age too much,
I will awake beside the one I love.

I will never walk away from love.
When I find it,
I will cradle it as if it was my child!

Thank you so much,
For everything you all have done.
I'm sure I will be thanking my
PA and best friend

A little more when my book hits the stores!

Once white porch

**Rumbling outside his head.
I must read, I must write.
If I'm not in before
you close your eyes...
Dream of me tonight.
The tree is showing its age,
Two rocking chairs.
Only the one now rocks alone.
Memories of an old man,
Leaves from the tree
Covers the once white porch
Time has passed without my
permission.
Memories is all I have
as my time begins to fade.
The screen door brushed
against what was, as it shut.
Looking back at the memories
of this old house and us.
Mom and dad loved each other
so much, now it's time to take
their memories home with us.
Their story will be told,
as dad, would have wanted it so.**

Bound

My hands,
bound
My mind blinded
by the darkness.
My soul,
captured by the universe.
The stars,
my guards.
My escape is not
Without flaws!

Tears

With every tear I shed
a thousand years of love.
With every moment
my heart grows cold
like the snow.
Has love forsaken me?
Why?
What have I done?
Love too much,
or always in the right place,
Wrong time?
Everywhere I look
I see those in love.
I look down at my hand,
And still it's empty
like the day before.
Some know not what they have,
till what they had is gone.
My heart has always picked the wrong ones.

King of the mountain

I sit on top my mountain
overlooking those below
wondering what they're
doing, as I wait for my love.
The birds are so loud,
I can't hear my own thoughts.
I feel as if I live in a rain forest,
but trust me I'm not.
Just a little town upon the
Rivers edge,
surrounded by very large hills,
and steep valleys
Nonetheless, I'm all alone
as I wait for my time
to hit the road.
I miss my life traveling far and near,
But not nearly as much as I miss her.
For I love her dear,
and this she knows.
I have even heard her say so.
Still I sit upon my throne,
on top my mountain all alone.

Perfect

Young, tender and sweet.

The perfect contour
of each cheek.

Lace on cotton,
looking so delightful,
riding high,
a beautiful sight,
for all to see.

Skin so soft,
so perfect,
one touch,
please?

Eclipse

Fire burnt bright
beyond the night.
The hours of darkness
hid the light.
A beautiful sight,
it truly is.
The golden colors
now turned black.
The darkness seems
to always follow me.
I thought the night
was supposed to be
calming!
It seems to only
haunt my dreams!

□

I know you love me

You Are Never Alone
Sh... Don't say a word,
You know I love you,
you are my perfect little boy.

Wipe your tears son,
I'm not far away!
I never stopped loving you,
It's just not my way!

My tears fall heavy when
I think of you.
Not a day goes by
that you're not in my heart.
I blame myself for us being
So far apart.

I too suffer from an empty heart.
There is no scarier place to be,
Than a blacken place where love
Use to be!

When you need me most,
go to that quite place where no one knows.
The one where you will find me most!
And one day soon, this is where you
will find me every day!

This will be a spot
just for the two of us to talk.
I love you son, and yes I know, shh..
I know you love me too!

Man in love

Man in love
as time grows
dark and weary,
my passion burns
deep down for
the woman of my
dreams.
Oh my love,
come let me
hold you for
eternity!
As the darkness
turn to light,
my passion for you
will creep up like
a thief in the night
sweeping you
off your feet.
As I set here
looking out my
window knowing
you can't see me

my heart starts to
burn down deeply...
Oh God hear my cry
I need you by my side...
But I'm not a patient man...
Oh my dear I wish you
were here!

Prisoner in my own head

A prisoner in own my mind.

This place is a prison,
my voice is the only
way to escape!

My soul and my body
slowly withering away!

My once positive thoughts
now soil the ground
beneath my feet with negativity!

My heart once beat
to the sound of the
little children.

Now only beats to the
Sound of my prison door
closing behind me...
□

The one that got away

To the one that touched
my heart.
Our love will always be
Strong.

No matter how far apart
you will always be
In my heart

The way you stared at me
Pierced a hole through
My Soul

Forever you will be
The only one
To have touched me.

Till we meet again,
I wish you well.

May my love guide you
Where ever
you decide to dwell

The Monster is dead

Shh… Don't let him hear you…
No…!
Found and bound by my feet!
Thump…! Thump…! Thump…!
My head playing music off the stairs.
I look over at my Malin, hide…!
Boom…! Boom…! Boom…!
Went my head off the floor.
I scratched and Clawed my way to the door!
Its claws pierce my skin,
as it yanked me back in.
It rend my clothes to pieces.
I was beaten, bruised, broken!
My Malin forced to watch,
As I lay naked upon the floor!
My body brutalized beyond recognition.
If that wasn't enough!
It began dragging me by my hair,
it threw me over the arm of the chair.
I looked over at my Malin…
Close your eyes!
Then the monster raped me
in more ways than you can image!
Through sweat, blood and tears,
I held on for my Malin.
My eyes weary, my body numb!
I have forgotten
what it was like to be loved!
Bang…! Bang…! Bang…!
I heard, then I felt the weight of the world
Falling upon me…!
My little warrior, my Malin-saved me!
He truly is my Malin,
The Monster is DEAD!!

Naked Souls

Naked souls, flow free into
the night, ever loving
in every flight.

Darkness growing cold
devouring everything in sight.

Without the light, we fade
into the darkness
without a fight.

Screams from within
those before who we
dare not mention,
scratching and clawing
Trying to find a way out!

Naked souls have no
Rights, the darkness
Wins every time.

Free

The darkness roars from within,
let me out as it screams.
Shall I listen or just ignore?
For every time, I open the door
all hell breaks loose,
but no more.
I am finely free
Never to be dangled by a string!
My soul is one with life.
I see more clearly now,
that I have opened my eyes.
Voice to one another and set
yourself free
Don't listen to the darkness,
it only wants one thing.

Confused

Is it real or is it not?

It's a long way to go,
if you don't know?

Red is rare,
as it beats like a drum.

Nerves of steel,
they are not.

What is real?

What is hot?

How far will you go?

Do you know?

Dazed

**Lost,
With no words
to say.
Then found,
I will not be.
Wondering unseen,
as I walk between,
the living and dead.
Dazed I truly am.**

My Mad House

Welcome to my
mad house...
Twisted minds
crazy thoughts
who's to blame,
who's is not?
They watch you
from the shadows.
They watch your
every word.
They think
they own you!
They think
their superior.
They thought
wrong!
I am the only
twisted mind
with crazy thoughts!

Little Princess

**One that smiles,
each and every day...
Never to let you go,
even when you say...
I don't need you,
please go away...
She knows,
when you're happy ,
and when you're sad...
She will always be there,
even when you're mad...
When you feel like giving up,
she will never let you down...
As beautiful as can be,
but never will she use
it to get her way...
When you yell help,
she is the first one you will see...
As time goes by
things will never change...
For Daddy's Little Princess
she will always remain..**

Woe

**Woe is me,
my mornings
slow to start.
Noises I hear,
mine they
are not.
No way,
this morning
is mine.
Give it back
and try
one more time?
Disrespectful,
others are!
A cup of coffee
would've done
the job!**

One day soon

**One day soon my arms,
Will be the last arms to hold you.
My lips only you will taste.
My blue eyes will never go to waste,
For when you go off to work,
Your beautiful face will be
A mire reflection of what I see,
When I look in the glass
That looks back at me.
Not a day will pass that I don't
Embrace you when you laugh,
When you smile, or when we kiss!
Your love is what I miss,
The soft touch of your lips,
And knowing you will always
Love me till the end!
"Love with NO end"**

Emptiness

Lamp post
Shining through
A darkened window
Streets empty
A black room
I once lived
Beating red
Love once was
Now darkness lies

Roaming Soul

Lost Soul roaming alone
Forest dark but,
her home as she
Walks out of the light
Into dark unprotected night
Looking for her love
□

Yesterday's gone

Sway to and fro
like the soft winds.
In the summer time
whisk, blissfully, with
no patience.
Calming pools without
a ripple.
No stone tossed by a
little one with freckle's.
It's a sweet summer treat,
but no kids playing in the streets,
on such a beautiful day.
Technology has scared
Mother Nature away.
As she hangings her head
In shame.

Stressful Times

**Twisted, head hanging low.
Too heavy to sit on the shoulders
of the man it use to know.
Seems like life's stress and
pressures have it earth bound.
Ah... What would it take to
make him rise again?
The weary and tarries of the earth,
can bound a man to the dirt!
He is a good man, please help,
please! I want to lift his spirit once again!
Let us strengthen him from within,
then his shoulders to hold his head.
Who would care so much to help
a fallen man?
The woman that believes in him,
and that will love him till the end!
Fallen he may be but,
to rise again he will...**

□

Chaos

**To be lost,
in a world of CHAOS!
Frozen in time,
to recapture youth.
Youth forgotten,
by the BODY!
Still trapped,
in the MIND,
is memories!
Love, lust and hunger,
brought forth,
the DESTRUCTION and DECEIT!
What you are,
or should be is to not to let others,
control your DESTINY!
KISMET should be,
of your own doing!
The bottom of life,
is nothing more,
than a second chance at life.
Choice,
or what you choose is your own.**

PROVIDENCE!

**To WASTE an opportunity,
is to shame!
For many would EXTERMINATE,
for a second chance at life!
To feel SHAMED or WRONGED,
for the way your lives have turned out!
Is nothing more
than the CRIES of a child,
WITHOUT guidance,
from those whom know,
where you are coming from!**

To Taste Desire

**Wanting her is a needed
desire.
Her long hair,
gives me something to hold onto.
Her eyes,
beautiful beyond compare,
lost in a stare.
Come with me,
dance in the fire.
The moon,
will be our light.
As I lay you down,
without being wed.
Don't close your eyes just yet,
I want you to see our first kiss.
Ah… your innocent's,
I'm about to feast upon.
A much-desired taste,
I so have acquired.
For my efforts, won't go unheard.
For your taste is much required,
On my tongue is where it's desired.
I thirst for your love,
For I couldn't live,
without you in my arms.**

Beautiful Babies

Beauty, I held in my hands
Three times in my life as a man
Now they are all grown up
With little beauties of their Own.
I get to see them when the kids drop by
The little ones like to run and hide
Seems like yesterday
When dad told me this day
would come.
It wasn't too long ago
I too was in your shoes.
It's the cycle of life son
this is just how it's done.
Grandpas gone and it
won't be long and I'll be
right behind him.
It's the cycle of life,
never forget me.

Simple Love

**Love, the true,
essence of a flower
opening
on a sweet summer morning.
A butterfly opening
its wings for the first time.
A soft wind
neither here, nor there
or from anywhere.
Blows everywhere
Ah… Love, it's the little
Things we simply over look.
A soft kiss
A pleasant good bye
Or maybe just good night
I remember when love was
Simple, a kiss and hug was
Essential, I love you, before leaving.
And I love you when I get home.**

Unwanted

Voices rumble inside my head
I can't make out what they are saying
Come close my dear let me hear you
To be told so many things
All at once has me confused
My head is spinning
What do I DO
Get out of my head for this is where I live
If I need you I will ask
Don't get your hopes up
I started long before most have
The train is moving, you weren't invited
My life is just getting started
I have new friends
A new game, this game is winning
Turn around and walk away
For your not wanted anyway
They all want to ride your train
When they think you're going places
Should have got aboard before
the train left the damn station
I don't have time for someone that
didn't believe in me in the first damn place
So keep your ass moving the other way
Be gone as some of my friends would say
This life I choose wasn't easy
I told you that, you didn't believe me
And I don't give a shit
There are those that wouldn't trade me in
It took me years to get where I am
So don't think you getting in here that easy
Life is about challenge

I had to face them all before getting into the

world I now call home.
Here is where I turn my back
for I don't know you anymore more!

Lost inside my head

Some say they are here to listen,
yet when truly needed
they're always busy.

Why can't I see passed the pain?
present, past or future,
it's all the same.

I've ask for god's help, Pained by fate,
I can't escape
my head is spinning I know I need help.
There's so much darkness
in my mind, my thoughts are
troubled all the time.

like my dad use to always say,
there will come a time
when he will stop listening
to our cry's.

I know I need help,
help I need,
yet I will never get on my knees.
because I am fine or is this just a lie?

Tired of Lies

Into the night, lost from sight
Blind because I can't see
for the light has forsaken me
I am bond to my destiny
for my life is laid out in
front of me.

Do I dare question my fate
is this for me to hate?
So many questions unanswered
as my head continues to blister.
Does anyone even care anymore
or is life just another closed door?

I'm tired of all the hiding,
lying is such a game
that always causes pain.

If you don't want,
then please, speak up
I'm not a toy for you to play with.
Just hang me from a tree and be
done with the thought of me.
The night is closing in around me
my light burnt out.

Lost in life

I saw my heart pass
as I looked out my window
through the rain
into the puddles
as it floated by.
I felt empty as the strong winds
from the storm blew
taking my soul with it.
All I have left is hope.
Fear settled in
for the first time.
My body, my dreams,
my mind, are not mine
for the very first.
Let me close my eyes
let me see the truth
for the first time.
Let tears fill my eyes!

Regrets

Time is ticking.
Lost in thin air.
I thought my troubles
where behind me,
but in fact they are not.
The color grey
starts to blind my way.
Decades of trying
to right my wrongs,
has lead me to many mistakes.
My troubles haunt me.
I wish they would just go away.
My heart keeps pounding.
Its feels like rage.
Please someone help me,
I'm so afraid

Touched

Touched deeply
And completely
Her love is now his
Over time they searched
Through life's
Unforeseen journeys
Even from afar he could feel
her in his heart.
Driven by destiny
The two will be merged as one.
On the day of one's birth
Even though they
Were miles a part
Their love couldn't
be torn.

Gone

**Long been gone,
heart sore and tore.
As it tarries in pain,
dangling in front of me.
The thought of emptiness,
leaves me but a husk.
My love gone from me,
she took her love,
her clothes,
her everything.
how could this be?
Lifeless wings
have taken her from me.
Lost in sorrow,
tears flooding my heart,
so much pain rends me apart.
Looking toward the sky,
Wondering, watching,
For my love to come back to me.**

Living the Moment

Love is absent where pain now lies
At less I'm no longer empty inside
But my heart no longer beats
Just a pounding pain in my chest
Death has possessed me
Everything I touch turns to ash
Her sinful thoughts and evil deeds
Will be the end of me
Now all that follows is the darkness
in which my soul belongs
To fade away and never be seen
Even when she lays next to me.
Cold nights,
yet still a blanket is my only friend.
Someone come and hold me
It's been so long.
I'm afraid I won't remember how
All I want is to be loved,
Was that too much to ask?
I guess I'll never know,
For she just walks passed,
As if I'm not here, how sad.
I feel as if I'm just
living in the moment.

The Hunger

There is a hunger burning deep inside!

A hunger that makes me want to run and hide!

A hunger I cannot fight!

You know of the hunger

in which I speak.

Time is ticking

You watch and see!

I've keep it at bay

But no more will it stay!

My eyes are burning

My hands sweat

My muscles twitch

As the hair on the back

Of my neck stands!

My knee fall forward

My feet go back

My hands hit the ground

RUN!

It's too late the hunger is back!

Ripple

A ripple in life's grand design

Left a tear somewhere in time

Things have changed

And we know not why

Looking out my window

Watching the red rain

The blue grass has now changed

I believe I'm going insane

We have no control

Life is making the choices for us

We just have to pick which journey

Is to be ours for this is a

new beginning for us all

Lost

Shattered minds

Liquid Dreams

Thoughts astray

Beneath my feet

Nothing more

Than puddles of defeat.

Tears flow through

The shutters where I blink.

As I watch my dreams

Flow into the streets.

My flesh wet

From where I weep.

I must ask, does this have to be?

My Story

From the being of my time

My heart has been broken

Eyes full of tears

Loneliness filled the air

Mistakes made

That lead me astray

Searching for love

But I knew not what love was

The feel of a woman was all I knew

But she or they would soon

Break my heart in two

Three decades later

And I'm still afraid

just like that little boy

all because nothing has changed

only gotten worse.

Till one day

Something happened to me

God must have gotten tried

Of my struggles

And sent me an Angel

Now Introducing a Guest Poet:

Jasmine Barry, Jasmine is a very close friend of mine. I have the upmost respect and love for Jasmine, her words hold meaning. I hope you enjoy them as I do.

Childish Games

Freaking childish games you play!

Grow up and take a look around,

Life is more than fantasy!

You need to start living in reality!

You took my youth and wasted it!

I am sick of trying to make you face it!

This is over here and now,

Your tears, nothing but, a fake excuse

To keep me here, for you to make me a slave!

Grow up and face it,

Your stupid shit I can take no more!

I want a life full of fun and happiness.

You were the stupid one,

I'm now wiser and it's a fact!

You're a child I took vows to raise,

Well that ends now,

I am no longer in a haze!

The Soul Weeps

Tears are a sign of our souls weeping

They fall from our eyes,

Like rain drops from the skies.

Sometimes it is happiness,

Sometimes it is sorrow,

Just know that it will be ok tomorrow.

Tears are something

One cannot borrow or buy.

Tears are earned by actions and lies!

Never deceitful or continuous betrayal,

Those are the worst things you can do!

Is lying to yourself part of your game?

If so then I should warn you

that life is unfair.

Karma will get you when you are not looking,

So make those special people priority

For moments are lost in the blink of an eye

As the tear falls those seconds are lost!

Wiped off to be flung out like the trash,

You can't ever get them back.

So cherish every moment with the ones you love,

For moments like this are one in a million.

Don't wait until it is too late,

And the soul is weeping.

ABOUT THE AUTHOR

I started so long ago, sixteen I believe the story goes. I wanted to be a song writer for my dad, but in his eyes my words were poetry not song. I went on to write hardcore rock for a bubby in a high school band, but no more than a few before moving on.

Years went by where I only worked on my art, given the words a break from my heart. Lacking the ability to edit I felt as if my words wasn't worth it. So, like Rip Van winkle, I closed my eyes for decades before rejoining the world of poetry.

www.ingramcontent.com/pod-product-compliance
Ingram Content Group UK Ltd.
Pitfield, Milton Keynes, MK11 3LW, UK
UKHW041915190726
13854UKWH00003B/1258

9 781387 024841